THE WORLD OF PONT

PONT

Pont, whose real name was Graham Laidler, was born in 1908 in Newcastle-upon-Tyne. He was educated at Trinity College, Glenalmond and then trained as an architect in London gaining an A.R.I.B.A. Because of ill health he turned to drawing cartoons, his first contributions in Punch appearing in 1932. It was in 1936 that *The British Character* series began giving immense pleasure and amusement. In 1938, *The British Character* was issued in book form and edition after edition were sold. *The Times* wrote prophetically ''Pont's drawings will not date . . .'' Pont died in 1940 at the early age of 32 years.

*By the same author
and available from Element Books*

THE BRITISH CHARACTER

The World of PONT

With an Introduction by
RICHARD INGRAMS

*"Now don't go walking in all those pools, Penelope,
there's a good girl."*

A Nadder Book
ELEMENT BOOKS LTD

A Nadder Book

This edition first published by Element Books Ltd 1983

Cover design by Humphrey Stone

Printed and bound by
Biddles Limited, Guildford, Surrey

ISBN 0906540 23 2

The illustrations in this book
are reproduced by permission of Miss Laidler
and the Proprieters of *Punch*

CONTENTS

*"I'm sorry, Miss Heslop, but your Botany Hour always
seems to sap my vitality."*

INTRODUCTION

by

RICHARD INGRAMS

The writer T.H. White once complimented Graham Laidler (Pont) on his sense of humour. "I do not try to draw funny people" the artist replied "I have no sense of humour. I try very hard to draw people exactly as they are." His success in doing this helps to explain his continuing popularity now more than forty years after his death. Looking at these wonderful drawings, we, the middle class English, can still recognise ourselves, our families, our friends and neighbours. Anyone who lives as I do in a house full of old beams, too many dogs, rows of well-thumbed detective stories and smoking open fires will feel immediately at home in the Pont atmosphere. If you are a commuter you will salute as a familiar figure the fierce city man who illustrates the "Love of Travelling Alone"* and who glares out into the train corridor with his umbrella and brief case laid across the vacant seats, defying anyone to enter the compartment. Which husband does not know only too well the suicidal figure with her head sunk in her hands above the caption "Absence of ideas for Meals"?* My own particular favourite, with whom I especially identify, is the man in the drawing called "Disinclination to Go Anywhere". He sits slumped in a comfortable armchair while his wife, who has

*Published in *"The British Character"*, Element Books

got someone on the other end of the phone asking them to dinner or drinks, gazes at him with a look of real desperation in her eyes. That man is me, and I agree with Pont that there is nothing funny or exaggerated about him. He perfectly illustrates the description of his fellow-countrymen by Sydney Smith: "There is nothing which an Englishman enjoys more than the pleasure of sulkiness – of not being forced to hear a word from anybody which may occasion him the necessity of replying. It is not so much that Mr Bull disdains to talk, as that Mr Bull has nothing to say. His forefathers have been out of spirits for six or seven hundred years and seeing nothing but fog and vapour he is out of spirits too; and when there is no selling or buying, or no business to settle, he prefers being alone and looking at the fire."

Graham Laidler was born in Newcastle on Tyne in 1908, the son of Gavin Laidler owner of a painting and decorating business. He was educated at Newcastle Preparatory School and later at Glenalmond in Perthshire. His father died in 1921 when Graham was thirteen and his mother let the large family house, 6 Osborne Avenue, Jesmond, and thereafter lived with her son and daughter Kathleen in a variety of addresses in the South of England, before they finally settled in the village of Jordans near Beaconsfield in Buckinghamshire. Nearby lived two maiden aunts, non-identical twins, who ran a domestic science school at Seer Green.

Graham started to draw at the age of about six, covering little sheets of writing paper with figures of horses and soldiers. He always wanted to be a cartoonist but, there not being much money in the family, was persuaded when he left school to train as an architect. In 1926 he entered the London School of Architecture in Bedford Square where he studied for five years. This was not time wasted for in addition to the purely architectural work, Laidler was given drawing lessons and went to life classes to draw the nude model – though he told his sister ''I only ever got as far as her feet.''

Laidler was a tall, very good-looking, rather shy young man. Even in 1939 his appearance was so youthful that he was refused admission to the Casino in Nice. A contemporary at the School of Architecture Professor Robert Goodden writes: ''As a student he was delightful company, quiet and softspoken mostly but quick to see the funny side of anything that had a funny side and very adroit in expressing in a word or two whatever he made of it so that we were all dissolved in laughter as soon as he had spoken. I think his great gift of expressing his own humorous observation of human nature in line drawings which expressed the characters of others so economically and gaily (traditional meaning of that word, not today's pilfering of it) must have escaped into marginal comments straying onto his sheets of architectural drawings, because I do remember that it was no surprise to find that within a year or two of leaving he had turned himself into the most enjoyable contributor to *Punch*, although so far as one knew he had been serious in his choice of the architect's profession.''

The change to cartooning took place towards the end of his time as an Architectural student. In 1932 he became increasingly ill and was found to be suffering from a tubercular kidney. After an operation at the London Hospital he was advised to give up office work and to spend his winters abroad, preferably in the mountains. He had already been contributing a strip cartoon to *Woman's Pictorial* and in 1932 had his first drawing accepted by *Punch*, subsequently becoming a regular contributor. In the end the editor E.V. Knox put him on a contract to draw exclusively for *Punch* – an arrangement otherwise unheard of. Not all the readers, however, thought so highly of him, one woman claiming that her daughter of six could do better. "In that case" Knox replied "I should be very glad to see some of her work". For his part Laidler never regretted his change of occupation. He once said he thought the cartoonist's life was better for his health; he felt a bit like an office boy who any day might get the sack and that the consequent uncertainty was good for him.

At the same time he threw himself into life, determining to do everything in his power to keep well. He had already travelled in Germany and Italy – he acquired his nickname 'Pont' in Rome when he styled himself Pontifex Maximus and the girls he was travelling with the Vestal Virgins – in 1933 he went to Switzerland, partly for treatment, then to Austria. His health began to recover and he was soon well enough to ski and go for long walks. In 1936 he visited Norway and Sweden and the following year he sailed to New York and travelled across America, spending several months on a ranch in Arizona – "America is just what you expect" he wrote home to his mother "Everyone rushing to get nowhere and everything around – buildings, bridges etc – built for use with no idea of beauty, but it is enormously interesting nevertheless. The poverty and squalor, the fabulous riches. It's all quite mad."

Pont was methodical and industrious. Wherever he went he found time to do drawings for *Punch*. He never stopped observing. Quiet and unobtrusive, he seemed to notice everything about people – the clothes, the gestures, the expressions on their faces "You miss so much just walking down the street" he scolded his sister. In particular he observed, though never without affection, his fellow Englishman in all his glory. In 1934 he began the series in *Punch* known as the British Character – later the title of his first book (published in 1938) – though the word British was a misnomer. The people were very definitely English. They were the sort of people he had come across in his sojourns with his family in Bucks; or the English tourists abroad, women with vacant faces, men with old school ties and moustaches, insisting on fresh air in trains and bacon and eggs for breakfast, defiantly refusing to speak the lingo – men wonderfully oblivious of their own absurdity. There was however nothing cruel in any of Pont's drawings. His observation was sharp but its strength lay in its never-failing spirit of good will. It would have amused him to know that during the war the Germans used his drawings in occupied Holland to make anti-British propaganda; which perhaps goes to explain why the British and Pont have ever since been popular with the Dutch.

Because of his early death, some critics have been tempted to conclude that Pont was cut off in his prime and died with his promise unfulfilled. It is not a view that I myself can share. During his brief career he was exceptionally prolific, producing over 400 cartoons for *Punch*, more than enough to fill five small books, two of which were published posthumously. It amounted to an oeuvre that many artists who made old bones would envy, culminating in his early wartime drawings all of which seem to sum up better than anything else the improbable spirit of 1940 – the fierce middle-aged woman confronting the heavily armed German soldier advancing across her lawn "How *dare* you come in here" or the impassive cloth-capped pipe-smokers listening to the German propaganda broadcast on the pub radio – "Meanwhile, in Britain, the entire population, faced by the threat of invasion, has been flung into a state of complete panic. . . ." Whenever social historians want to recapture the mood of that historic time they will turn to these immortal cartoons.

Pont died of polio, after an illness of only a few days, on the 23rd November 1940. It has been said by people who see only his brief career, his illness, his short love affair with a girl whose parents forbade her to marry a non-Roman Catholic, that his life was unhappy, even tragic. Nothing could be wider of the mark. Pont had a melancholy side. His great friend Robert Hunt remembers him as at times a rather sad man who reminded him of another great comic artist, Edward Lear. But there was nothing in the least bit tragic about him. "He possessed" another friend wrote in the RIBA journal at the time of his death "a love of life that led him to a wide range of activity, from writing and painting to gardening and ski-ing, and a gentleness and forgiving spirit in the face of wrong that was at times unbelievable." In 1937 Pont himself wrote to his aunt May, who had been arguing with him about religion: "Please don't be sorry for me. Look upon me as a rather fortunate fellow. I've had some experience of being ill and knowing what it feels like to be sure you're going to die. Well, I'm the richer for that. Life is, contrary to my earlier ideas, intended to be lived and you must enjoy as many experiences as you can grasp or you haven't truly lived. Even the ones that hurt aren't to be avoided, and only the fools are anything but wiser for them . . . I'm sorry for people who get everything their own way . . . I have a growing faith in life, and by living I think one gets an idea of God, someone *real* – not a vague shadowy old Gentleman to whom we mumble the Lord's prayer on our knees as part of the ritual of preparing for bed, like toothbrushing.''

February 1983

THE BRITISH OBSERVED

THE BRITISH CHARACTER
Skill at Foreign Languages

THE BRITISH CHARACTER
Absolute Indispensability of Bacon and Eggs for Breakfast

THE BRITISH CHARACTER

Importance of the Morning Bath

THE BRITISH CHARACTER
Lack of Confidence in the Driver

THE BRITISH CHARACTER
Interest in Natural History

THE BRITISH CHARACTER
A Tendency to be Conscious of Draughts

THE BRITISH CHARACTER
*The Tendency Among Week-end Guests to
Leave Things Behind*

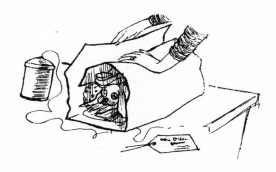

THE BRITISH CHARACTER
A Tendency Not to Return Borrowed Books

THE BRITISH CHARACTER
A Tendency to Put Off till the Last Minute

THE BRITISH CHARACTER
Importance of Not Taking Precedence at Doorways

*"And the trouble with that young man is that he's got nothing
whatever in his head but new ideas."*

THE BRITISH CHARACTER
Firm Conviction that Things Aren't What They Were

"Oh, how d'you do. I've always detested your pictures."

THEATRESCAPE WITH CRITIC
"This new comedy at the stagehouse hasn't got a smile in it."

THE BRITISH CHARACTER
Ability to be Ruthless

THE BRITISH CHARACTER
Disinclination to go Anywhere

THE BRITISH CHARACTER
Attitude Towards Sunday Mornings

THE BRITISH CHARACTER
A Tendency to Despair on Monday Mornings

THE BRITISH CHARACTER
Exaltation of Freedom

THE BRITISH CHARACTER
Importance of The Twelfth of August

THE BRITISH CHARACTER
Love of The Open Fireplace

THE BRITISH CHARACTER
Tendency to Keep Out of Foreign Politics

THE BRITISH CHARACTER

A Keen Curiosity About the Future

THE BRITISH AT WAR

*"Gosh! Aren't you sick and tired of all these silly
jokes about the black out."*

POPULAR MISCONCEPTIONS
How to Fill the Troops with Keenness

*"I remind you of who?" I said. "And
then I knocked the blighter down."*

"*. . . Meanwhile, in Britain, the entire population faced by the threat of invasion, has been flung into a state of complete panic . . . etc., etc., etc.*"

"My Lord, the bicycle's at the door."

"Good Lord! He can't speak English."

"I'm not going to have people turning round and blaming ME if we don't win this damned war."

"*Austria, Czechoslovakia, Poland. And now, dammit, Hunting.*"

"Come, come, Mr. Brewis, you aren't going to ration ME."

"How dare *you come in here."*

"At least, Sir, you can scarcely deny that dictators are human beings."

"What I said was, 'My husband is leaving on a frantically hush-hush mission to Belgrade on Tuesday!'"

"I'm perfectly aware of that."

"Haven't you got a nice kiss for the Commander?"

"It never fails to amaze me how these taxi-drivers find their way about at night."

POPULAR MISCONCEPTIONS

POPULAR MISCONCEPTIONS
England

"Please, Mother, can I go to the pictures?"

POPULAR MISCONCEPTIONS
After Dinner in the Kitchen

"Oh, no, Madam, we wouldn't have anything in your size."

POPULAR MISCONCEPTIONS
The People Behind

*"But, sir! I told you yesterday I didn't know
Queen Elizabeth's dates."*

POPULAR MISCONCEPTIONS
The English Channel

*"Spread yourself out more, Daisy, or they'll
get past."*

POPULAR MISCONCEPTIONS

England in Spring

''What *man with a beard gives you the creeps?*''

POPULAR MISCONCEPTIONS
Life in Scotland

"Club Sandwiches."

POPULAR MISCONCEPTIONS
Life when Mother was Young

"My parents have a theory about bringing up children."

POPULAR MISCONCEPTIONS

Life when Father was a Boy

"Master George would prefer rice-pudding."

POPULAR MISCONCEPTIONS
Life Among the Really Rich

"I am sure none of you boys are responsible for putting the frogs in Matron's bed last night."

POPULAR MISCONCEPTIONS
Life in the Flat Above

"Not eating your fat – and millions *starving in Russia!"*

"Not eating your fat – and millions *starving in Russia!"*

POPULAR MISCONCEPTIONS
Bureaucrats at Work

POPULAR MISCONCEPTIONS

Life in the Secret Service

THE BRITISH WOMAN

"Watch closely now, Janet, and see how I turn out a blancmange."

"Why *must I* go and change my shoes,
and socks, Mother?"

THE BRITISH WOMAN
Half-an-hour's Rest After Meals

"Good heavens, Mother, what have you been doing to your hair?"

"Don't you think you could try *to take it in, you stupid man, that I'm only a learner?"*

"Is it cold this morning, boys?"

"Look, everybody, isn't it splendid, he saved me from drowning."

*"Once upon a time there was a teeny-
weeny little fairy. . . ."*

The "Please, Mother, will you tell me a story?" peril.

"My *cook makes a* delicious *tomato soup.*"

The ''I Can Do Anything Except Cooking'' Situation.

"Now don't you dare come in here and tell me you think you've got measles."

"*Miss Sylvia asked me to inquire, your Ladyship, whether she need wash this morning in view of her having taken a bath only yesterday evening.*"

"Now, now, your ladyship, remember the time-table – Kissing from 5.30 to 6."

"Did you say chocolate éclair OR meringue?"

"*I don't wish to seem to be interfering or anything
Mildred, but do you not think perhaps you've got your
oven a wee bit high?*"

*"Sir Thomas and Lady Partingdale, Lord Crodleigh and the
Bishop of Hopton."*

85

"*Of course I* entirely *agree with you. But which crisis is it you mean?*"

CONVERSATION PIECE

"*I* insist *on my children always sleeping with the windows open.*"

*"If you take my advice you won't go upstairs to her.
There's nothing wrong; she's only crying because she
just wants someone to go and talk to her."*

"It's not a bit of use asking me, my dear man; I can't see a thing."

"Mr Sparks, dear . . . longing to meet you."

THE BRITISH CHARACTER
A Tendency to Leave the Washing Up Till Later

"Please, something which won't make me think. *"*

CHILDREN'S VESTS, CARPETS,
BOXING GLOVES, STAIR RODS, BEES,
STEAM ROLLERS AND MACHINE GUNS

THE BRITISH CHARACTER
Absence of Decision

"But of course dear. Mother's frantically interested in everything you say."

"Oh, for lunch, *was it?"*

"Why of course, Mrs. Harrison, it's perfectly *all right about bringing with you your sister* and *her husband* and *their daughter* and *their two sons* and *their son's friend who have arrived unexpectedly."*

"Bring her another duck, waiter."

"Now don't go and get into a flap or anything, Mother, but Joan's broken her arm."

THE BRITISH WOMAN
Cult of the Christmas Re-union

*"Mummy, before any one invented
trains, did you – ."*

"And now in return we want you to promise to bring all your family to spend the day with us on Saturday week."

"Please don't hesitate to say if you prefer your coffee white. It will be no trouble at all for me to get the car out and drive over to the dairy for some milk."

"I am ever so sorry, but Mrs. Tweedie never touches soups."

" – and at home it's always 'mind you don't get your feet wet'!"

"*And now I suppose you're going to tell me that the last one's gone
and there isn't another until next Thursday.*"

THE BRITISH MAN

*" . . . and the taxpayers will shoulder
these new burdens with light hearts,
thereby showing the world, etc.,
etc., etc."*

WINTER EVENINGS AT HOME
Dressing Up

"Herbert, don't disturb your Father!"

THE BRITISH MAN
The Gentlemen were all at School together

"I ate sixty-four chocolate biscuits."

AT HOME
The Amateur Inventor

"And here's one of him taken at Eastbourne when he was five."

"Good gracious!"

*"Dear, dear. There's nothing for it but a long
rest and plenty of cigars."*

"Go and find the General, Peters, and tell him that if he doesn't come in to lunch instantly he shan't have any."

*"And now, Harrison, kindly tell cook to come up and see me
for a moment."*

"Please don't disturb yourselves, my good people. My friend and I are only studying conditions among the rich."

AT HOME
The Millionaire

*"I wonder if you realise, Wilson, that this egg is too lightly
boiled."*

AT HOME
The Epicure

AT HOME
The Bachelor

"Now I would like to organize the whole World. . . ."

AT HOME
The Author

AT HOME
Genius

AT HOME
The Neurotic

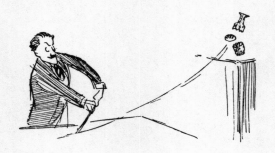

AT HOME
The Cricket Enthusiast

"Just talk to me on any subject – except hunting."

"There's a most unusual-looking bird on the lawn."

WINTER EVENINGS AT HOME
A Game of Hide-and-Seek

To the end of the Beach –

– and back

"Don't blame me, Mr. Croodleton, if Alfie's given you the sack. I told you right at the beginning that boy had push."

"But remember, the more business improves now, the further it will have to fall when the next crash comes."

"You see, doctor, I've never had an illness in my life, so sometimes I get frightened that it may mean there's something wrong."

Tendency among Business-men to believe in doing Business over Lunch

"I suppose you know you're doing that all wrong."

"Ho, so you don't believe that every man should have the right to express his own opinions freely, don't you?"

"Harold, do you notice anything different about the room?"

"Darling, you must PROMISE me you won't catch cold."

Available again

THE
BRITISH
CHARACTER

Studied and Revealed by
PONT

With an Introduction by
ALAN COREN

''Pont is undeniably a genius` . . .''
ALAN COREN

ISBN 0 906540 25 5 *Hardback* £4.95
ISBN 0 906540 23 2 *Paperback* £2.50